Y0-CAA-462

THE CALLS OF
FROGS AND TOADS

0 11557 02968 0

THE CALLS OF
FROGS AND TOADS

Lang Elliott

NatureSound Studio

STACKPOLE
BOOKS

Copyright © 2004 by Lang Elliott

Published by
STACKPOLE BOOKS
5067 Ritter Road
Mechanicsburg, PA 17055
www.stackpolebooks.com

All rights reserved, including the right to reproduce this book or portions thereof in any form or by any means, electronic or mechanical, including photocopying, recording, or by any information storage and retrieval system, without permission in writing from the publisher. All inquiries should be addressed to Stackpole Books, 5067 Ritter Road, Mechanicsburg, PA 17055.

Printed in China

10 9 8 7 6 5 4 3 2 1

This is a revised and expanded edition of the book originally published in 1992 by NatureSound Studio and in 1994 by NorthWord Press.

Pencil drawings by Cynthia J. Page

Photo Credits: Lang Elliott: cover, 12, 13, 14, 15, 17, 18, 19, 20, 21, 22, 24, 25, 28, 29, 30, 31, 32, 33, 35, 36, 37, 38, 39, 40, 41, 42, 43, 44, 45, 48, 49, 50, 51, 52, 53, 56, 57, 60, 61; Jeff LeClere: 16; James C. Godwin: 23; James E. Gerholdt: 34

Library of Congress Cataloging-in-Publication Data

Elliott, Lang.
  The calls of frogs and toads / Lang Elliott.
    p. cm.
  ISBN 0-8117-2968-0
  1. Frog sounds. 2. Toad sounds. I. Title.
QL668.E2 E58 2004
597.8'1594—dc22

2003022284

Contents

Credits and Acknowledgments

*T*he Calls of Frogs and Toads *was created, narrated, and produced by Lang Elliott, owner and operator of NatureSound Studio.*

The Sound Recordings: The majority of recordings used in this work were collected in the field by Lang Elliott of NatureSound Studio and Carl Gerhardt of the University of Missouri. Additional recordings were provided by Ray Anderson, Bill Evans, Tom Johnson, Ted Mack, Paul Moler, Bill Turcotte, the American Museum of Natural History, the Borror Laboratory of Bioacoustics at Ohio State University, the Florida State Museum of Natural History, and the University of Texas Memorial Museum. All recordings are copyrighted by the individuals or institutions that made them.

Acknowledgments: Special thanks goes to Carl Gerhardt for sharing his recordings and providing expert advice concerning the development of this product. Bill Evans and Liz Maynard provided invaluable personal support throughout. I wish also to thank Ted Mack and Greg Budney for the hours we shared listening to frog and toad sounds in the field.

This guide is dedicated to Dean Metter of the University of Missouri, who introduced me to the joys of frog and toad study in his herpetology course in the late 1960s. Interestingly, the subject of my term paper for his course was "The Calls of Frogs and Toads." Voila!

Introduction

The frogs and toads (order Salientia) are a diverse and successful group of amphibians with nearly 3,700 species worldwide. About 95 species are native to North America, with about 42 of these ranging east of the Great Plains. The 42 frogs and toads covered in this guide fall into five taxonomic families; these are described in detail later.

The difference between frogs and toads is not clear-cut. In general, the typical toad has dry, warty skin, short legs, a chunky appearance, and moves with short hops. Members of the family Bufonidae (the true toads) have these qualities. In contrast, the typical frog has smooth, moist skin, a slender profile, and long legs adapted for leaping. Members of the family Ranidae (the true frogs) fit this category. Confusion arises because species in the other three families often show a combination of toadlike and froglike characteristics.

Life History and Breeding

*T*he life cycle of frogs and toads in our region is illustrated below. Most species breed in the spring or early summer, often with the onset of warm, rainy weather. Males gather in ponds, pools, and other wet areas. They make their presence known with loud advertisement calls that seem to attract females (and possibly males) of the same species to the breeding chorus.

When a receptive female approaches a male, he responds by climbing on top of her back and clasping her tightly with his front legs, a posture known as amplexus. During amplexus, the female lays eggs and the male sheds sperm on them as they emerge.

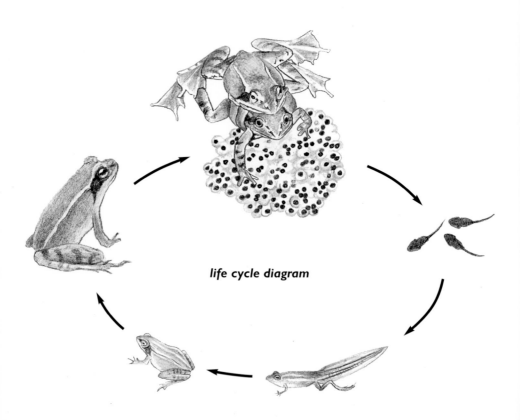

life cycle diagram

Some species are explosive breeders, responding immediately to favorable weather and completing their breeding season in a matter of days. Other species, especially those whose adults are largely aquatic, have a prolonged breeding season that may extend for several months or more. Certain southern species breed in spurts, becoming active whenever the weather conditions are favorable. Other southern frogs breed only during warm spells in the winter.

Eggs are laid in the water, sometimes attached to vegetation, and undergo development without any parental care. After a variable period of time (a week to a month or more), the eggs hatch into aquatic gilled larvae known as tadpoles or pollywogs. Tadpoles feed on algae and other aquatic debris. They eventually sprout legs, absorb their tails, and emerge as miniature adults referred to as froglets or toadlets. Growth occurs slowly and some species take several years to reach breeding size. Depending on species, adults may be aquatic, terrestrial, or arboreal, except during the breeding season, when nearly all return at least temporarily to the water.

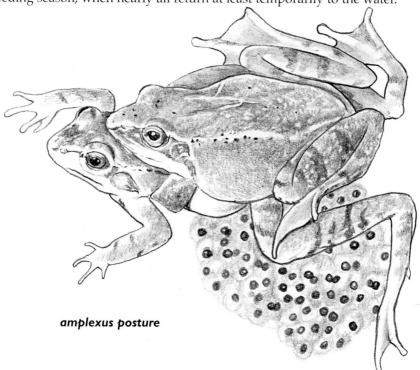

amplexus posture

Call Types and Their Functions

The prominent calls made by males during the breeding season are termed advertisement calls because they advertise the presence of breeding males. The calls of each species are usually distinct, and it is generally assumed that individuals are attracted to the calls of their own species, rather than other species, when migrating toward breeding sites (although surprisingly few scientific studies have actually demonstrated this point).

Advertisement calls may have several functions. It is likely that they attract receptive females, but they may also attract other males to the breeding chorus (there is some evidence that large choruses of calling males are more effective at attracting females than small choruses). They may also serve a territorial function by repelling other males from the area surrounding a calling male. This is especially true in aquatic species like Bullfrogs, where males occupy and defend stable territories that they use for feeding as well as breeding.

There are numerous accounts of closely related species producing hybrid offspring. When mature, male offspring produce hybrid calls that are intermediate in character to the calls of the parental species.

If one listens to single-species choruses, one may notice that males in close vicinity to one another often do not call at random. Two, three, or four males may sometimes alternate their calls with rhythmic regularity, possibly to reduce call interference and allow approaching females to hear them more clearly. A contagious effect may also be heard. After periods of quiet, one individual may suddenly begin calling and the others quickly join in. The group choruses actively for a period of time, and then they all become quiet again. Interactions like these occur more rarely between species.

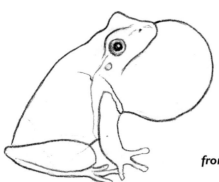

front pouch

Males possess vocal pouches that they inflate while calling, adding loudness and resonance to their calls. Treefrogs, true toads, and members of other groups typically possess a spherical, thin-walled pouch (figure 3) that is inflated like a balloon. Many true frogs have paired vocal pouches (figure 4), which extend outward to each side. Bullfrogs and other species have less-defined, thick-walled pouches (figure 5). When calling, their throats bulge outward from one side of the mouth to the other.

thin side pouches

The physical dynamics of calling differ among species, but a general pattern is often followed. First, the male draws air in through his nostrils to inflate his lungs and vocal pouch. He then seals off his nostrils, creating a closed system, and makes sound by rapidly forcing air from his lungs into

thick side pouches

his vocal pouch, or back and forth between them, passing the air through his larynx (voice box) in the process. His pouch usually remains inflated while he is calling, although it may be partially collapsed when air is moved to the lungs prior to each call. The pouch is not fully deflated until the calling sequence is over and the nostrils are once again opened.

Females that approach a chorus may breed at random with the first male they encounter, but there is evidence that females of some species choose a male based on his calling ability, his location in the chorus, or the quality of his calling territory.

In the early stages of the breeding season, especially among toads, males often mistake other males for females and climb atop them to attempt amplexus. The male being mounted responds with release calls, a series of chirping sounds that are usually accompanied by rapid vibrations of the abdomen. This alerts the male on top that a mistake has been made and encourages him to dismount (although mounted males sometimes must wrestle their way free). It is thought that the abdominal vibration stimulates release, with the audible calls being of secondary importance. In many species, males respond aggressively if other males approach too closely and begin calling. In such situations, the resident male produces distinctive aggressive calls, which communicate his aggravation. If the other male does not retreat, a fight may ensue, with one male physically ousting the other from the immediate area.

When the breeding season is over, nonaquatic species quit calling, leave their wetland breeding sites, and quietly pass the rest of their active season in arboreal or terrestrial habitats. At this time, especially during humid or rainy weather, individuals may call intermittently from trees or shrubs for no apparent reason. These calls, which are often hoarse or raspy versions of advertisement calls, are loosely termed rain calls, and their exact function is not known. Rain calls are common among treefrogs. It is possible that such calling is a response to hormonal changes, especially in northern species such as the Spring Peeper, which undergo physiological changes in the autumn prior to winter dormancy. However, this does not explain why southern species such as Squirrel Treefrogs commonly give rain calls before, during, and after the breeding season.

If one walks along the shores of lakes and ponds during the summer months, alarmed frogs periodically leap from the shoreline, squeaking loudly before splashing into the water. Such alarm calls are commonly given by members of the family Ranidae, many of which spend a great deal of time waiting for insect prey at pond's edge. The function of these calls is unknown, but they do seem to alert other frogs to approaching danger and they may startle predators. When seized by a predator, a variety of species emit loud, wailing screams or cries, often with their mouths open. These distress calls may induce a predator to drop the prey, allowing for a quick escape.

Learning to Identify Frog and Toad Sounds

This audio guide presents the calls of forty-two native species of frogs and toads found east of the Great Plains (that is, east of a line running from western Louisiana to western Ontario). While it can help you identify frog and toad sounds even without seeing the creatures themselves, it should not take the place of actual outdoor observation. The best way to learn is to view the soundmakers in their breeding habitats so that images as well as sounds become imprinted in your mind.

The descriptions that follow are coordinated with what you hear in the reference section of this guide (compact disc tracks 1–42). The recordings of each species are combined in sequence to produce reference soundprints. The date, location, and recorder of each field recording is listed at the end of the species descriptions.

Track 43 is a narrated introduction to the calls of frogs and toads. This track is 32 minutes long and features examples of advertisement calls, hybrid calls, release calls, aggressive calls, rain calls, alarm calls, distress calls, call alternation, and much more.

The Calls of Frogs and Toads

Ranidae: The True Frogs

There are about twenty-seven species of true frogs in North America, with fourteen occurring east of the Great Plains. All species are members of the genus *Rana*. Body format is that of the "typical frog," with slim waist and long legs. All species show prominent webbing between the toes, an adaptation for swimming. This family includes our largest frogs (Bullfrog, Pig Frog, and River Frog), as well as the spotted "biology lab frog" (the leopard frogs). Many species are aquatic or semiaquatic as adults, although some are terrestrial.

Northern Leopard Frog

Notes: Our largest native frog, grows to 6 to 8 inches length. Ranges throughout eastern and central North America, with patchy distribution in the West. Aquatic during active season; found in lakes, ponds, and streams. Avoids temporary bodies of water.

Voice: Advertisement call of male is a series of loud, resonant bass notes sounding like *rumm . . . rumm . . . rumm . . .* or else a stuttering *ru-u-u-umm . . . ru-u-u-umm . . .* (often verbalized as "jug-o-rum" and somewhat resembling the bellowing of a bull). These calls function both as breeding calls and territorial calls. An abrupt, spitlike *phphoot!* is given during aggressive encounters. Calls from shallow water along shorelines or from offshore patches of floating or emergent vegetation. May be heard from May to August in the North; late winter to autumn in the South.

Recordings:
1. Large chorus; 6/7/89; Tompkins Co., N.Y.; Lang Elliott.
2. *Phphoot!* call; 4/20/89; Bradley Co., Ark.; Lang Elliott; N. Cricket Frogs prominent in background.

Notes: Up to 6 inches in length. A southern, aquatic species, restricted to coastal plain regions from South Carolina to eastern Texas. Abundant in Florida. Breeds in marshes, lakes, and swamps.

Voice: Breeding call of male is a low-pitched, guttural, piglike *grunt,* often given in a series: *grunt-grunt-grunt . . .* The number of *grunt*s in a series is related to temperature. A rapid series of up to eight or ten *grunt*s may be given during warm and humid periods. Large choruses produce a steady roar. A spitlike *phphoot!*—similar to that of the Bullfrog—is given during encounters. Usually calls from offshore vegetation, sometimes while floating in water. Heard from April to August.

Recordings:
1. Long *grunt*-series; 4/22/89; Cameron Co., La.; Lang Elliott; S. Cricket Frogs in background.
2. *Grunt* and *phphoot!* calls; 4/26/89; Wakulla Co., Fla.; Lang Elliott; crickets prominent in background.

Notes: Grows to about 4 inches long. Primarily aquatic in habits. Abundant throughout the East along the edges of ponds, lakes, streams, and other permanent bodies of water.

Voice: Advertisement and territorial call of the male is an explosive, throaty *gunk!* or *gung!* resembling the sound made by plucking a loose banjo string. Calls often delivered in a series that drops slightly in pitch and volume: *Goonk!-gunk!-gunk!* During encounters may give several stuttering, guttural calls of *ru-u-u-u-ng . . . ru-u-u-u-ng . . .* followed by a single staccato *gunk!* When aroused, may also give an abrupt hiccup sounding like *iCUP!* When approached, leaps from shoreline and squeaks in alarm just before hitting water: *eeek!* Breeds from spring to late summer; calls from shoreline or from floating vegetation.

Recordings:
1. Typical *gung!* calls; 7/28/88; Tompkins Co., N.Y.; Lang Elliott.
2. Stuttering calls and *iCUP!*; 5/27/87; Tompkins Co., N.Y.; Lang Elliott; Spring Peepers in background.
3. *Eeek!* alarm calls; 9/15/91; Tompkins Co., N.Y.; Lang Elliott; crickets trilling softly in the background.

4. Wood Frog — *Rana sylvatica*

Notes: Up to 3 inches long. A northern species, found in the Northeast and upper Midwest of the United States, and throughout most of Canada and Alaska. Terrestrial outside the breeding season; prefers moist, wooded areas.

Voice: Advertisement call of male is a ducklike quacking or cackling, usually consisting of several harsh notes given in rapid succession, *cack-a-hack* or *cack-a-hack-a-hack*, often delivered in a repetitive fashion: *r-r-racket, r-r-racket, r-r-racket* . . . Breeds after first spring rains, sometimes with snow still on ground. Males gather in woodland pools and roadside ditches and call excitedly while floating in the water. Breeding lasts only a week or two if suitable weather persists.

Recordings:
1. Small chorus; 3/30/88; Tompkins Co., N.Y.; Lang Elliott.

Notes: Up to 3 inches long. Named for minklike odor that is given off when handled. A northern aquatic species; breeds during summer months in northwoods ponds, lakes, and streams. Found from Minnesota to Maine and throughout much of eastern Canada.

Voice: Primary advertisement call is a series of about four sharp raps, *cut-cut-cut-cut*, which resemble the sound made by striking two sticks together. Aroused individuals produce a rolling, stuttered series of calls: *grrruut-grrruut-grrruut-grrruut* . . . Calls from late June into August. Calling peaks in early July, especially in the middle of the night, when huge choruses can be heard rapping away in boggy northwoods ponds.

Recordings:
1. Typical calls; 6/24/89; Franklin Co., N.Y.; Lang Elliott; Green Frogs, Spring Peepers, and Bullfrog in background.
2. Group chorus; 7/4/91; Franklin Co., N.Y.; Lang Elliott; Green Frogs in background.

6. Carpenter Frog   *Rana virgatipes*

Notes: Reaches nearly 3 inches in length. A southern species, restricted to coastal plain regions from New Jersey to northeastern Florida. Prefers sphagnum bog habitats, but also found in lakes and ponds.

Voice: Advertisement call is a distinctive series of sharp, doubled rapping notes that sound like two carpenters hammering nails slightly out of synch: *cu-tuck, cu-tuck, cu-tuck, cu-tuck* . . . May be heard from spring to late summer.

Recordings:
1. Advertisement calls; 3/30/89; Chesterfield Co., S.C.; Lang Elliott.

Notes: Grows to about 2 inches long, the smallest member of the family Ranidae. A recently discovered species with a very restricted range. Found only in cool, clear freshwater seeps and boggy areas in Okaloosa and Santa Rosa Counties of the western panhandle of Florida.

Voice: The male's advertisement call is a series of sharp, slightly rattled or garbled notes that drop in volume from beginning to end: *currt-currt-currt-currt-currt* . . . Soft, garbled notes are sometimes given singly. Males also produce a loud, single-noted *PIT!* that appears to be an aggressive call given during territorial encounters. Males may be heard calling from April through August.

Recordings:
1. Typical calls, garbled notes, and *PIT!* calls; 5/1/92; Santa Rosa Co., Fla.; Lang Elliott; S. Cricket Frogs and Green Frogs in background.

Notes: Grows to 4 inches or longer. A spotted frog, closely resembling other leopard frog species. Found throughout much of the southern Great Plains; ranges into parts of Missouri, Iowa, Illinois, and Indiana.

Voice: Advertisement call consists of two to four throaty, *chuck*ing notes repeated several times in rapid succession: *chu-hu-huck, chu-hu-huck, chu-hu-huck* or *hi-hi-hip, hi-hi-hip, hi-hi-hip*. Each outburst of *chuck*s rises slightly in pitch and ends with an accent. A soft *grunt* may terminate a series. Males also produce squeaking notes reminiscent of the sounds made by rubbing one's finger across the surface of an inflated balloon. Breeds in early spring, following the first warm rains.

Recordings:
1. Typical calls; 5/20/92; Saline Co., Mo.; Carl Gerhardt; N. Cricket Frogs and Gray Treefrogs prominent in background.

9. Southern Leopard Frog *Rana sphenocephala*

Notes: Up to 5 inches long. The common "spotted frog" of southern swamps and marshes. Found throughout the southern states. Ranges north to Missouri, Illinois, and Indiana; along the Atlantic coast to Long Island. Often wanders away from water into grassy or weedy habitats.

Voice: Advertisement call, which is repeated several times in rapid succession, consists of a series of five or more guttural *chuck*ing notes that are delivered as a stutter that is usually too fast to count: *chu-hu-hu-hu-huck, chu-hu-hu-hu-huck, chu-hu-hu-hu-huck* . . . At low temperatures, *chuck*s at slow rate and may sound like Plains Leopard Frog, but has more *chuck* notes in each series. Squeaky *grunt*s are often given at end of a *chuck* series. Breeds in spring in the North, but may be heard throughout the year in the South.

Recordings:
1. *Chuck*s and *grunt*s (cool weather); 3/4/89; Harrison Co., Miss.; Lang Elliott; Spring Peepers in background.
2. Warm weather example; 5/5/88; Leon Co., Fla.; Lang Elliott; Green Treefrogs and S. Cricket Frogs in background.

Notes: Up to 5 inches long. Ranges across northern United States and into Canada. Breeds along vegetated margins of ponds, lakes, and streams. A common spotted frog popularly known as "meadow frog" due to its habit of visiting grassy meadows and lawns.

Voice: Breeding call of male is an extended, rattling snore lasting about three seconds or longer and usually followed by various *grunts* or *chuck*-ing notes. An early spring breeder; may be heard calling both day and night during the first warm spells of spring.

Recordings:
1. Snores and *grunts*; 4/19/71; Tompkins Co., N.Y.; Lieberberg and Loker (provided by Carl Gerhardt). Spring Peepers in background.

Notes: Grows to 3 inches or longer. A spotted frog, recognized by two distinct rows of squarish spots running down its back (leopard frogs have roundish spots arranged irregularly). Found throughout much of the East, but absent from the extreme Southeast. Breeds in lakes, ponds, streams, bogs, swamps, springs, and in the twilight pools at cave entrances. Also frequents grassy areas away from water.

Voice: Advertisement call is a harsh snore of about a two-second duration (the snore of the Northern Leopard Frog is more extended). Males sometimes call while submerged. Garbled, throaty notes are occasionally given singly, perhaps during aggressive encounters. Breeds in the spring; may be heard calling in early summer in northern areas.

Recordings:
1. Typical snores; 4/21/87; Tompkins Co., N.Y.; Lang Elliott; Spring Peeper in background.
2. Snores and single garbled note; 4/2/89; Rutherford Co., N.C.; Lang Elliott; trickling spring in background.

Notes: Up to 4 inches long. A nocturnal species, named for its habit of taking shelter by day in burrows of other animals, especially Gopher Tortoises. Found in dry, sandy habitats of coastal plain regions from North Carolina to Mississippi. Breeds in nearby ponds and swamps. An isolated population known from a single site in southern Mississippi is considered by some biologists to be a separate endangered species, the Dusky Gopher Frog, *Rana sevosa*.

Voice: Advertisement call is a deep, roaring snore lasting about two seconds. *Chuck*ing notes may also be given. Calls in late winter or early spring over most of its range, but may be heard in summer in Florida. Large breeding choruses are of common occurrence.

Recordings:
1. Typical calls; 3/19/69; Chatham Co., Ga.; Carl Gerhardt; S. Leopard Frog, S. Chorus Frog, Little Grass Frogs in background.
2. Active chorus; 2/21/75; Putnam Co., Fla.; David Lee; S. Leopard Frog and crickets in background.

Notes: Grows to almost 4 inches long. Habits similar to the Gopher Frog. Prefers moist prairies, pastures, and meadows where it takes shelter by day in crawfish burrows or the burrows of other animals. Ranges from Texas and Louisiana north to Missouri and Illinois.

Voice: Advertisement call is a low, rumbling snore usually lasting less than one second: *wwwahhhhhh*. May precede snores with soft, stuttered *chuck*-ing notes. During aggressive encounters, makes abrupt, nasal notes: *wah! . . . wah! . . . wah! . . .* May be heard calling from early spring to early summer.

Recordings:
1. Snores, *chuck*s, and *wah!* calls; 4/12/72; Boone Co., Mo.; Carl Gerhardt; American Toads, W. Chorus Frogs, and S. Leopard Frog in background.

Notes: Grows to 6 inches long. A southern frog of slow-moving rivers, swamps, and ponds. Found in coastal plain regions from southeastern North Carolina to northern Florida, southern Alabama, and southern Mississippi. Uncommon over most of its range.

Voice: Advertisement call is a low, rumbling snore lasting from one to three seconds and trailing off in volume at the end. Two or three snores are usually given in succession. Unlike Gopher Frogs, River Frogs generally do not call in choruses, and the calls of lone males are easily overlooked. Breeds from April or May through summer.

Recordings:
1. Typical snores (three excerpts from long recording); 5/24/85; Columbia Co., Fla.; J. C. Hancock (provided by Paul Moler); Green Treefrogs and S. Cricket Frogs in background.

Hylidae: Treefrogs and Allies

A diverse family, with about twenty-five species in North America, approximately twenty of them found in our region. Most are small (less than 3 inches long), slim, and have long, slender legs. Our native species fall into three genera: *Hyla* (treefrogs or treetoads), *Pseudacris* (chorus frogs), and *Acris* (cricket frogs). Members of the genus *Hyla* have prominent adhesive toe pads, an adaptation for an aboreal life among trees or shrubs. The other genera have reduced toe pads and are semiaquatic or terrestrial in habits.

Gray Treefrog

Notes: Grows to about 2¹/₂ inches long. Normally bright green, but may change color to dull yellow or gray. An abundant southern treefrog that frequents a variety of habitats. Found throughout the South, but ranges northward into southeastern Missouri, and along the Atlantic coast as far north as Delaware.

Voice: Advertisement call is a harsh, nasal *quank-quank-quank-quank* . . . repeated about once per second. From a distance, calls may sound bell-like, which accounts for the local name of "cowbell frog." Aggressive call given during encounters is a hoarse, garbled *quarrr-quarrr-quarrr* . . . that is harsher than advertisement call and repeated more quickly. Called "rain frog" because huge choruses erupt after warm rains. Breeds in still water swamps, marshes, and ponds.

Recordings:
1. *Quank* calls (two males counter-calling) followed by aggressive calls; 5/4/88; Leon Co., Fla.; Lang Elliott.
2. Group Chorus; 4/26/89; Wakulla Co., Fla.; Lang Elliott; Pig Frogs periodically call in background.

Notes: Grows to nearly 2 inches long. One of our most beautiful frogs (green above with white-bordered lavender stripes on each side). Has a very restricted distribution. Found only in pine barren habitats of New Jersey, the Carolinas, the Florida panhandle, and southern Alabama.

Voice: Advertisement call is a harsh *quok-quok-quok-quok* . . . that is very similar to the call of the Green Treefrog but somewhat more melodic and usually higher in pitch and repeated more rapidly (up to three calls per second). Can be heard calling from swamps, bogs, and shrubby areas where water seeps to the surface.

Recordings:
1. Typical *quok* calls; 5/10/92; Chesterfield Co., S.C.; Lang Elliott; Whip-poor-wills and American Toads in distance.
2. Fast-paced calling; 6/10/69; Bladen Co., N.C.; Carl Gerhardt.

Notes: Up to 2³/₄ inches long; one of our largest native treefrogs. Found primarily in coastal plain habitats from North Carolina to eastern Louisiana. Isolated populations occur in Kentucky, Virginia, Maryland, and New Jersey. Secretive outside the breeding season. Known to climb trees, but may also burrow into soil to escape heat.

Voice: Advertisement call is a hollow, resonant *ooonk*, repeated about once per second. From a distance sounds like the hollow barks of a hound dog. Gives a different call from trees or shrubs: a harsh, barking *arrk-arrk-arrk-arrk* . . . Breeds from spring to early autumn in shallow ponds and cypress swamps.

Recordings:
1. Typical calls; 7/27/67; Evans Co., Ga.; Carl Gerhardt; Pine Woods Treefrog, Squirrel Treefrog, and S. Cricket Frog in background.
2. Chorus; 3/27/89; Marion Co., Fla.; Lang Elliott; S. Cricket Frog in background.
3. Rain call; 7/24/67; Chatham Co., Ga.; Carl Gerhardt; Pine Woods Treefrog, Squirrel Treefrog, and S. Cricket Frog in background.

Notes: Grows to about 1¹/₂ inch long. Able to change color from green to brown, with or without spots. A southeastern coastal plain species found from Virginia to Texas. Sometimes an arboreal feeder, but often found on ground near decaying stumps or logs.

Voice: Advertisement call is a harsh, nasal, and buzzing *rrrraak-rrrraak-rrrraak-rrrraak . . .* repeated at a rate of around two per second for long periods. Tree call (rain call) is a series of very raspy, squirrel-like notes that are repeated about once every second for about 15 to 20 seconds. Breeds from late spring into summer in temporary ponds and ditches.

Recordings:
1. Advertisement calls; 7/22/69; Chatham Co., Ga.; Carl Gerhardt; Eastern Narrow-mouth Toads in the background.
2. Rain calls (dawn); 4/30/89; Leon Co., Fla.; Lang Elliott; bird sounds faint in background.

Notes: Grows to about 1³/₄ inch long. Spends much of time high in trees, especially pines, where it feeds on small insects. Its reddish-brown color provides camouflage against brown pine bark. Prefers pine forest habitats in coastal plain regions from Virginia to eastern Louisiana.

Voice: Advertisement call is a rapid, long-continued series of raspy notes resembling the sound made by a riveting machine, or else someone tapping wildly at a telegraph key: *dik-dik-dikadikadikadikadikadikadikadika* . . . Calls more or less continually at the breeding site. Gives shorter and more slow-paced versions from trees or shrubs, especially during rainy or humid periods. Breeds from late spring through summer in ditches, pools, and small ponds.

Recordings:
1. Typical call-series (close-up); 6/24/71; Jasper Co., S.C.; Carl Gerhardt; S. Cricket Frogs background.
2. Breeding group; 5/30/75; Richmond Co., N.C.; Donald Borror.

Notes: Grows to almost $2^1/2$ inches long. Individuals can change color from gray to green. Found throughout much of region, but distribution is patchy and generally nonoverlapping with look-alike species *Hyla chrysoscelis* (the two species were long considered one and are best told apart by their calls). Spends most of its time above ground, looking for insects in trees and shrubs.

Voice: Advertisement call is a short, melodic trill lasting about one-half second and repeated every few seconds. Pulse rates of trills vary with region (slow in the East and upper Midwest, faster in the southwest part of range). When approached by another calling male, responds with squeaky chirps or yelps that signify aggression. Breeds from late spring into summer in ponds and pools surrounded by shrubs or trees. In summer, may trill from trees or shrubs.

Recordings:
1. Slow pulse rate trills; 5/26/92; Tompkins Co., N.Y.; Lang Elliott; Spring Peepers and Green Frogs in background.
2. Aggressive chirps with trills; 5/86; Tompkins Co., N.Y.; Lang Elliott.
3. Fast pulse rate trills; Grayson Co., Tex.; Carl Gerhardt.

Notes: Grows to almost 2$^{1}/_{2}$ inches long. Individuals can change color from gray to green. Found throughout much of region, but distribution is patchy and generally nonoverlapping with look-alike species *Hyla versicolor* (the two species were long considered one and are best told apart by their calls). Spends most of its time above ground, looking for insects in trees and shrubs.

Voice: Advertisement call is a short trill, like that of *Hyla versicolor* but harsher in quality. Trills of eastern populations have a slow pulse rate; western populations have a fast pulse rate. In aggressive situations, responds with squeaky chirps like those of *Hyla versicolor*. Breeds from late spring into summer in shallow ponds, pools, and ditches surrounded by shrubs or trees.

Recordings:
1. Slow pulse rate trills (eastern); 8/3/69; Bryan Co., Ga.; Carl Gerhardt.
2. Fast pulse rate trills (western); 7/2/89; Payne Co., Okla.; Carl Gerhardt; N. Cricket Frogs in background.

Notes: Grows to nearly 2 inches long. A southern species, found from Louisiana to Florida panhandle and north into South Carolina, Alabama, and Kentucky (absent from most of Florida). Spends time feeding quietly in trees or shrubs in wooded swamps and river bottoms. Little is known about its natural history outside the breeding season.

Voice: Advertisement call is a rapid series of ten to twenty melodic peeps lasting several seconds and sometimes varying slightly in tempo. During aggressive encounters, responds with a harsh trill given singly or in repetition: *prrreeeeek!* Breeds in ponds and pools or swampy areas, usually near rivers or creeks.

Recordings:
1. Chorus; 7/5/72; Jasper Co., S.C.; Carl Gerhardt.
2. *Peep*-series followed by aggressive calls; 4/23/69; Chatham Co., Ga.; Carl Gerhardt.

23. Spring Peeper *Pseudacris crucifer*

Notes: Grows to about 1¹/₂ inch long. Scientific name *crucifer* refers to cruci-fix-like "X" on its back. Widespread and abundant throughout the eastern half of the United States and southern Canada (but absent from southern Florida). Frequents wooded or brushy areas. Not often seen outside the breeding season when it looks for insects in shrubs, trees, or on the ground.

Voice: Advertisement call is a series of sharp, piercing birdlike peeps repeated about once per second or faster (but never as fast as calls of Bird-voiced Treefrog). Distant chorus may sound like the jingling of sleigh bells. Breeds in pools, ditches, and ponds, from spring to early summer in North and from winter to spring in South. Aggressive call is a short, stuttering trill, *purrrreeeek,* usually rising in pitch at the end. Rain call, given periodically from trees and shrubs in summer and autumn, is a repeated series of peeps or squeaks that are harsher and more dis-sonant than springtime advertisement calls.

Recordings:
1. Advertisement calls; 4/21/87; Tompkins Co., N.Y., Lang Elliott.
2. Chorus; 4/13/92; Tompkins Co., N.Y.; Lang Elliott.
3. Aggressive calls; 4/24/90; Tompkins Co., N.Y.; Lang Elliott.
4. Rain calls; 9/15/91; Tompkins Co., N.Y.; Lang Elliott.

Notes: Grows to over 1¹/₂ inch long. A coastal plain species, ranging from North Carolina to eastern Louisiana (absent from southern Florida). Terrestrial; lives in open grassy areas. May burrow for shelter.

Voice: Advertisement call is a metallic, piping *pip-pip-pip-pip-pip* . . . repeated at a rate of around two or three notes per second. Similar to calls of Spring Peeper, but more clear and bell-like, with notes repeated more quickly. Breeds from December through March, usually after rains. Calls from temporary pools or ponds and roadside ditches adjacent to open areas.

Recordings:
1. Typical calls; 1/27/67; Chatham Co., Ga.; Carl Gerhardt; S. Chorus Frogs in background.
2. Chorus; 1/11/75; Alachua Co., Fla.; David Lee; Spring Peepers and male cricket in background.

Notes: Grows to almost 2 inches long, the largest member of the genus. A species of the southern Great Plains. Ranges into western Arkansas and Louisiana, with isolated populations in cenral Illinois and southeastern Missouri (some biologists consider these isolated populations to be a distinct species, the Illinois Chorus Frog, *Pseudacris illinoensis*). Found in a variety of habitats, from woodland to open fields or meadows.

Voice: A series of clear, bell-like peeps, *pip-pip-pip-pip-pip* . . . sounding almost identical to the calls of the Ornate Chorus Frog. However, the ranges of the two species do not overlap. Breeds in ponds, pools, and ditches, from winter into spring, during or after rains.

Recordings:
1. Advertisement calls; 3/12/73; Scott Co., Mo.; Carl Gerhardt.

26. Little Grass Frog

Pseudacris ocularis

Notes: Less than ³/₄ inch long when full grown, our smallest North American frog. A southeastern species, found in coastal plain habitats from Virginia to Florida. A poor climber. Active during day in open grassy areas.

Voice: Advertisement call is very high-pitched and insectlike, consisting of an introductory note followed by a brief and rapid trill: *pt-zeee, pt-zeee, pt-zeee* . . . repeated once or twice per second. Chorus sounds like a large group of crickets. Breeds from winter into summer, with a springtime peak. Calls from flooded grassy meadows, roadside pools, and ponds with emergent grassy vegetation.

Recordings:
1. Typical *pt-zeee* calls; 6/11/73; Bryan Co., Ga.; Carl Gerhardt.
2. Small group; 7/17/67; Bryan Co., Ga.; Carl Gerhardt.

Notes: About 1¹/₂ inches long. A widespread chorus frog found throughout much of the East but absent from the Northeast, the Appalachians, and the extreme Southeast. Common in agricultural areas, where it breeds in roadside ditches and pools. Long considered to be a subspecies of the Western Chorus Frog, the southerly Upland Chorus Frog, *Pseudacris feriarum*, is now considered a distinct species, and so is the northerly Boreal Chorus Frog, *Pseudacris maculata*. Their voice, appearance, and habits are nearly identical to that of the Western Chorus Frog. Some biologists believe this group should be further divided to include the New Jersey Chorus Frog, *Pseudacris kalmi*. Because all these related species sound virtually identical, and their taxonomy is still being explored, they are treated as one group in this guide.

Voice: Advertisement call is a rapid series of metallic, *creek*ing clicks that rise in pitch, much like the sound made by rubbing a finger across the stiff teeth of a small comb. Calls are repeated every one or two seconds: *crrreeeeek . . . crrreeeeek . . . crrreeeeek . . .* Breeds from winter to spring in roadside ditches and other shallow water habitats, often adjacent to farmland.

Recordings:
1. Advertisement calls; 6/89; Clinton Co., N.Y.; Ted Mack.

Notes: Grows to 1¹/₄ inch long. A small, dark chorus frog with warty skin. A southeastern species, found in coastal plain regions from North Carolina to Mississippi, including all of Florida. Frequents a variety of habitats. Habits outside breeding season are little-known.

Voice: Advertisement call is a clicking *crrreeeeek*, which sounds almost identical to the call of the Western Chorus Frog. The two species are best told apart by anatomical differences, not by sounds. Breeds in winter, from November to April. Calls from grass at edge of water in roadside ditches, temporary pools, flooded fields, and so on.

Recordings:
1. Typical calls; 3/10/68; Chatham Co., Ga.; Carl Gerhardt.

29. Brimley's Chorus Frog *Pseudacris brimleyi*

Notes: Grows to about 1¼ inch long. Found in coastal plain habitats from Virginia to Georgia. Habits similar to those of other chorus frogs.

Voice: Advertisement call an upslurred *crrreeeeek*, much like those of the Western and Southern Chorus Frogs but more raspy in quality, of shorter duration, and with less differentiation between the clicks making up each call. Breeds from November to March or April in ponds, pools, swamps, and ditches.

Recordings:
1. Advertisement calls; 3/2/69; Chatham Co., Ga.; Carl Gerhardt; Spring Peepers in background.

30. Mountain Chorus Frog *Pseudacris brachyphona*

Notes: Grows to about 1¹/₂ inch long. Ranges throughout most of the Appalachian Mountain region from southwestern Pennsylvania to northern Georgia and Alabama. A terrestrial woodland species found in forested mountain habitats. Likened to a miniature Wood Frog.

Voice: Advertisement call is a harsh, raspy trill with an abrupt upslurred ending: *currrrrick!* or *zzzrrrick!* Lower in pitch and more raspy than calls of other chorus frogs and reminiscent of the calls made by Squirrel Treefrogs. Breeds from winter to spring in pools, ditches, ponds, or springs in forest or forest-edge settings.

Recordings:
1. Advertisement calls; 3/17/68; Dawson Co., Ga.; Carl Gerhardt.
2. Advertisement calls; 3/17/68; Dawson Co., Ga.; Carl Gerhardt; Spring Peepers prominent in background.

Notes: Grows to about $1^1/2$ inch long. A small, warty frog with nonclimbing habits. When disturbed, leaps an extraordinary distance for its size. Widespread and abundant throughout most of East and Midwest, but notably absent from the Northeast, the Appalachian Mountains, and the extreme Southeast.

Voice: Advertisement call is a vibrant series of metallic notes that sound like two small glass marbles being tapped together: *giiick-giiick-giiick-giiick-giiick-giiick* . . . Notes are usually given in a long series that starts out slow, speeds up in tempo, and then slows down at the end with extended notes. Has a vibrant quality because notes are slightly modulated or trilled. Breeds from late winter into summer. Calls from open or grassy edges of ponds, lakes, creeks, and swampy areas.

Recordings:
1. Typical call-series (daytime); 5/21/88; Stoddard Co., Mo.; Lang Elliott; Bullfrog and faint bird sounds in background.
2. Chorus; 5/1/91; Trigg Co., Ky.; Lang Elliott.

32. Southern Cricket Frog   *Acris gryllus*

Notes: Grows to about 1¹/₄ inch long. A southern species. Found from Virginia to Louisiana, primarily in coastal plain regions. Warty; looks like a small toad. Habits and appearance are both very similar to the Northern Cricket Frog.

Voice: Advertisement call is a series of about five to ten metallic, clicking notes. A series usually lasts less than 5 seconds and is given at a fairly even pace: *gick-gick-gick-gick-gick-gick-gick*. May be heard any month of the year, but breeds primarily from April through summer. Calls from floating vegetation or from shoreline in lakes, ponds, pools, and streams.

Recordings:
1. Advertisement calls; 7/11/89; Chesterfield Co., S.C.; Lang Elliott; Green Treefrogs and Green Frogs in background.
2. Chorus; 5/4/88; Leon Co., Fla.; Lang Elliott; Green Treefrogs in background.

Bufonidae: The True Toads

There are about twenty-one species of true toads in North America, with seven species in our region. All are members of the genus *Bufo*. These are the toads with which most of us are familiar. They are chunky in appearance and have warty glands and ridges on their skin. Especially prominent are the parotid glands, located on the back behind each eye. These contain irritating poisons that serve to discourage would-be predators. Toads are more resistant to dehydration than species in other families and may wander far from water. They prefer cool, damp, protected areas. Native species in our area range in size from $1^{1}/_{4}$ inch long (Oak Toad) to about 5 inches long (Gulf Coast Toad).

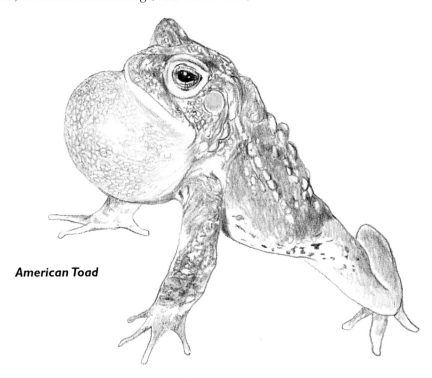

American Toad

33. American Toad — *Bufo americanus*

Notes: Grows to over 4¹/₂ inches long. A well-known "hop-toad" of yard and garden. One of the most common and widespread of eastern toads, but easily confused with Fowler's Toads, with which it hybridizes. Found throughout most of eastern United States and Canada but absent from the extreme South and Southeast. Frequents a variety of habitats, from urban and suburban areas to deep forest. Night-active; hides during day.

Voice: Advertisement call is a long, dreamlike, musical trill lasting from several seconds to 30 seconds or more (average duration around 10–15 seconds). Each male in a chorus sings at a slightly different pitch (1500–2000 Hz). Males alternate and overlap their calls in a pleasing manner. Hybridizes with Fowler's Toad. Hybrids produce a harsh trill that is intermediate in quality and duration between the typical calls of the two parental species. When mounted, males respond with distinctive release calls: throaty squeaks or chirps, often quickly repeated. Breeds in spring, April to June in the North and as early as January in the South.

Recordings:
1. Chorus; 5/10/89; Tompkins Co., N.Y.; Lang Elliott; Spring Peepers in background along with very soft release calls of toads.
2. Release calls; 5/18/89; Tompkins Co., N.Y.; Lang Elliott; Spring Peepers in background.

Notes: Grows to about 4 inches long. The common toad of the southeastern coastal plain region. Found from southeastern Virginia to eastern Louisiana. Primarily night-active.

Voice: Advertisement call is a trill of about 5 to 10 seconds in duration. Sounds similar to the call of the American Toad, but is not as melodic and is higher in pitch (2300–2500 Hz). In choruses, an audible dissonance occurs when loud calls of individuals overlap. Release call of male is a series of grating notes or chirps, usually accompanied by a barely audible low-pitched hum caused by vibrations of the midsection. Heard from March to June, especially after rains. Breeds in ponds, pools, and ditches, usually near forest.

Recordings:
1. Chorus; 5/3/92; Columbia Co., Fla.; Lang Elliott.
2. Release calls and vibrations; 3/4/89, Wakulla Co., Fla.; Lang Elliott.

Notes: Reaches nearly 5 inches in length, the largest native toad in our region (but note that the Giant Toad, *Bufo marinus*, a Central American species ranging into extreme southern Texas, may grow to a length of 9 inches or more). Found in Central America and eastern Mexico. Ranges north into Texas, southern Louisiana, and southeastern Mississippi, with isolated populations extending into Arkansas. Found in a variety of habitats from urban areas to coastal beaches and prairies.

Voice: Advertisement call is a low-pitched trill (1300–1400Hz) of about 2 to 6 seconds in duration. It is considerably lower in pitch than calls of American or Southern Toads. Breeds March through September in ponds, lakes, and roadside ditches.

Recordings:
1. Typical trills; Hancock Co., Miss.; Bill Turcotte.

36. Fowler's Toad *Bufo fowleri*

Notes: Grows to about 3½ inches long. Easily confused with American and Southern Toads and will hybridize with both. Found through most of eastern United States, but absent from parts of the Northeast, the Southeast, and the upper Midwest. The Fowler's Toad was formerly considered a subspecies of the more western Woodhouse's Toad, *Bufo woodhousii*. The Woodhouse's Toad, which ranges into western Iowa, Missouri, Arkansas, and Louisiana, has a nasal trill that sounds much the same as that of the Fowler's Toad.

Voice: Advertisement call is a buzzy, nasal trill lasting from 1 to 5 seconds: *waaaaaaaaaa!* Sounds somewhat like a baby crying. Calls of hybrids are usually intermediate in quality between calls of parent species, both in harshness and duration. Breeds mostly from February through May, but may be heard calling in summer from lakes, ponds, rivers, ditches, and pools.

Recordings:
1. Advertisement calls; 5/88; Wayne Co., Mo.; Ted Mack; N. Cricket Frogs, Gray Treefrogs, and S. Leopard Frogs in background.
2. Chorus; 4/30/91; Trigg Co., Ky.; Lang Elliott.

Notes: Grows to about 4$^{1}/_{2}$ inches long. A Great Plains species, ranging into our area in western Minnesota and Iowa, and along the Missouri River valley in Missouri. The common toad of grasslands and dry prairie. Night-active. Burrows for protection from heat and dryness.

Voice: Advertisement call is a loud, continuous, pulsating trill with a shrill, rattling, metallic quality: *chiga-chiga-chiga-chiga-chiga* . . . Reminiscent of the sound made by a pneumatic drill. Can be heard from a great distance; deafening at close range. Breeds spring into summer in rivers, ponds, ditches, and flooded areas.

Recordings:
1. Advertisement calls; 6/14/56; Traverse Co., Minn.; Univ. of Texas.
2. Chorus; 4/72; Shawnee Co., Kan.; Tom Johnson.

Notes: Grows to about $1^1/_4$ inch long. The smallest true toad in North America, often confused with young Southern Toad. An abundant southeastern species, found in upland pine or pine-oak woodlands in coastal plain regions from Virginia to eastern Louisiana. Commonly seen during the day. Burrows for protection during dry periods.

Voice: Advertisement call is a series of piercing, high-pitched tones or squeaks reminding one of the peeps of baby chickens: *peeee-peeee-peeee-peeee-peeee* . . . Higher in pitch and more drawn-out than calls of Spring Peeper or Bird-voiced Treefrog. Breeds spring through summer in pools, ponds, and ditches, especially after warm rains.

Recordings:
1. Advertisement calls; 6/21/72; Bryan Co., Ga.; Carl Gerhardt; Pine Woods Treefrogs and Barking Treefrogs in background.
2. Chorus; Harrison Co., Miss.; Bill Turcotte; Green Treefrogs prominent in background.

Pelobatidae: The Spadefoots

Spadefoots are a lesser-known group with a plump, "toady" appearance, but lacking prominent warts on skin. Seven species occur in North America. Three species are found in the East, although one is a plains species ranging only into the Missouri River valley. Spadefoots are distinguished by vertical pupils and a black, horny "spade" on the inside of the hind feet (an adaptation for burrowing). They are nocturnal in habits and remain underground for long periods, but venture forth on warm, humid nights. Both regional species are explosive breeders and respond instantly to warm, heavy rains. Males gather in shallow pools and breed within a day or two. Eggs transform to tadpoles and then toadlets in as little as two weeks' time.

Eastern Spadefoot Toad

39. Eastern Spadefoot *Scaphiopus holbrookii*

Notes: Grows to 3¹/₂ inches long. A burrowing species, rarely seen except during warm, rainy periods when it emerges to feed and breed. Often confused with true toads (look for vertical pupils). Primarily southeastern in distribution, but ranges northward into southern Illinois, Indiana, and Ohio, and along the coast north to Massachusetts. Prefers habitats with dry, loose soils. May cause allergic reaction if handled. Originally considered a subspecies of the Eastern Spadefoot, the Hurter's Spadefoot, *Scaphiopus hurteri*, is found in parts of Texas, Oklahoma, Louisiana, and Arkansas. Its habits and voice are basically identical to that of the Eastern Spadefoot.

Voice: Advertisement call is an explosive, nasal utterance, usually downslurred, and sounding like a person vomiting: *errrrrrah!* Has also been likened to call of an immature crow. Repeats call every 5–10 seconds. Breeds in temporary pools caused by heavy rains. Heard during summer in North and anytime during year in South.

Recordings:
1. Typical calls (close-ups); 3/12/73; Scott Co., Mo.; Carl Gerhardt.
2. Chorus; Harrison Co., Miss.; Bill Turcotte.

Notes: Grows to 2¹/₄ inches long. A Great Plains species ranging into our area along the Missouri River valley (with a small, isolated population in north-central Arkansas). Found in dry, sandy soils.

Voice: Primary advertisement call is a snorelike growl, repeated once every 1–2 seconds. It is higher in pitch and shorter in duration than the snores of leopard frogs or the Pickerel Frog. May also make a nasal bleat, similar to that made by the Eastern Spadefoot. Breeds in pools, ditches, and flooded areas in spring or summer, after warm rains.

Recordings:
1. Snorelike growls; 4/21/76; Howard Co., Mo.; Carl Gerhardt; W. Chorus Frogs and Fowler's Toad background.

Microhylidae: The Narrowmouth Toads

Seldom-seen, smooth-skinned toads with plump, swollen bodies, narrow heads, and pointed snouts. All have a fold of skin on the back of the head. Three species occur in North America. Two are found in the East but one is a plains species that barely ranges into the region; both eastern species are members of the genus *Gastrophryne*. Narrowmouth toads are very secretive in habits, taking shelter under objects or in burrows and only emerging during damp, warm nights. Both species breed in response to warm rains that may occur any time from early spring into autumn.

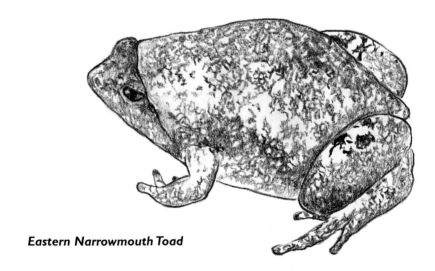

Eastern Narrowmouth Toad

Notes: Grows to about 1¹/₂ inch. A southern species, ranging from Maryland and Virginia west to Missouri and southward to the gulf states. Found in a variety of habitats. Extremely secretive in habits.

Voice: Advertisement call is a buzzy, nasal *waaaaaaaa!* lasting about one to several seconds. Sounds like the call of the Fowler's Toad, but is shorter in duration, more buzzy, and sometimes preceded by a soft squeak or peep. Aggressive call is a harsh, throaty *brrrrrrrrr*, repeated slowly. May be heard from spring to autumn, after heavy rains. Breeds in ponds, lakes, pools, and ditches.

Recordings:
1. Chorus; 7/23/73; Chatham Co., Ga.; Carl Gerhardt.
2. Aggressive calls; 7/23/73; Chatham Co., Ga.; Carl Gerhardt.

Notes: Grows to over 1$^1/_2$ inch in length. A southern Great Plains species that ranges into our region along the Missouri River valley in Missouri. Found in grassland and open woodland (and desert habitats in the West). Hides beneath objects or in burrows where it feeds on ants and other insects.

Voice: Advertisement call is nasal, buzzy bleat of 1–4 second duration that is preceded by a loud, high-pitched squeak or peep: *peep-waaaaaaaaa!* Call is easily confused with that of the Eastern Narrowmouth Toad, but the introductory peep is much louder. Breeds from spring to autumn after heavy rains.

Recordings:
1. Advertisement calls; 6/29/63; Grimes Co., Tex.; Univ. of Texas; Gulf Coast Toads soft in background.

Master List of CD Contents

Species numbers are equivalent to track numbers on the compact disc. Each species is identified by name and number on the compact disc before its sound repertoire is presented. Written descriptions of each animal's calls can be located with ease within this book by referring to the appropriate species numbers as listed below or as heard on the disc.

RANIDAE: THE TRUE FROGS

1. **Bullfrog**
   Large chorus
   Phphoot! call

2. **Pig Frog**
   Long *grunt*-series
   Grunts and *phphoot!* calls

3. **Green Frog**
   Typical *gung!* calls
   Stuttering calls and *iCUP!*
   Eeek! alarm calls

4. **Wood Frog**
   Small chorus

5. **Mink Frog**
   Typical calls
   Group chorus

6. **Carpenter Frog**
   Advertisement calls

7. **Florida Bog Frog**
   Typical calls, garbled notes,
   and *PIT!* calls

8. **Plains Leopard Frog**
   Typical calls

9. **Southern Leopard Frog**
   *Chuck*s and *grunt*s
   (cool weather)
   *Chuck*s and *grunt*s
   (warm weather)

10. **Northern Leopard Frog**
    Snores and *grunt*s

11. **Pickerel Frog**
    Typical snores
    Snores and single garbled note

12. **Gopher Frog**
    Typical calls
    Active chorus

13. **Crawfish Frog**
    Snores, *chuck*ing notes,
    and *wah!* calls

14. **River Frog**
    Typical snores (three excerpts
    from long recording)

HYLIDAE: TREEFROGS AND ALLIES

15. **Green Treefrog**
    Quank calls (two males
    counter-calling) followed by
    aggressive calls
    Group chorus

16. **Pine Barrens Treefrog**
    Typical *quok* calls
    Fast-paced calling

17. **Barking Treefrog**
    Typical calls
    Chorus
    Rain Call

18. **Squirrel Treefrog**
    Advertisement calls
    Rain calls (dawn)

19. **Pine Woods Treefrog**
    Typical call-series (close-up)
    Breeding group

20. **Gray Treefrog**
    Slow pulse rate trills
    Aggressive chirps with trills
    Fast pulse rate trills

21. **Cope's Gray Treefrog**
    Slow pulse rate trills (eastern)
    Fast pulse rate trills (western)

22. **Bird-voiced Treefrog**
    Chorus
    Peep-series followed by
        aggressive calls

23. **Spring Peeper**
    Advertisement calls
    Chorus
    Aggressive calls
    Rain calls

24. **Ornate Chorus Frog**
    Typical calls
    Chorus

25. **Strecker's Chorus Frog**
    Advertisement calls

26. **Little Grass Frog**
    Typical *pt-zeee* calls
    Small group

27. **Western Chorus Frog**
    Advertisement calls

28. **Southern Chorus Frog**
    Typical calls

29. **Brimley's Chorus Frog**
    Advertisement calls

30. **Mountain Chorus Frog**
    Advertisement calls
    Advertisement calls (Spring
        Peepers in background)

31. **Northern Cricket Frog**
    Typical call-series (daytime)
    Chorus

32. **Southern Cricket Frog**
    Advertisement calls
    Chorus

BUFONIDAE: THE TRUE TOADS

33. **American Toad**
    Chorus
    Release calls

34. **Southern Toad**
    Chorus
    Release calls and vibrations

35. **Gulf Coast Toad**
    Typical trills

36. **Fowler's Toad**
    Advertisement calls
    Chorus

37. Great Plains Toad
Advertisement calls
Chorus

38. Oak Toad
Advertisement calls
Chorus

PELOBATIDAE:
THE SPADEFOOTS

39. Eastern Spadefoot
Typical calls
Chorus

40. Plains Spadefoot
Snorelike growls

MICROHYLIDAE:
THE NARROWMOUTH TOADS

41. Eastern Narrowmouth Toad
Chorus
Aggressive calls

42. Great Plains Narrowmouth Toad
Advertisement calls

43. Narrated introduction to the calls of frogs and toads.
Includes high-fidelity audio examples of advertisement calls, hybrid calls, release calls, aggressive calls, rain calls, alarm calls, distress calls, call alternation, and mixed species choruses.

Frog and Toad Families: A Quick Reference

RANIDAE: THE TRUE FROGS
smooth skin
slim waist
long legs
webbed feet
mostly aquatic

HYLIDAE: TREEFROGS AND ALLIES
mostly small in size
long, slender legs
toe pads
terrestrial or semi-aquatic

BUFONIDAE: THE TRUE TOADS
chunky appearance
shorter legs
warty glands and ridges
prominent parotid glands
mostly terrestrial

PELOBATIDAE: THE SPADEFOOTS
distinctive vertical pupils
horny spade on inside of hind feet
chunky appearance
relatively smooth skin
terrestrial

MICROHYLIDAE: THE NARROWMOUTH TOADS
swollen bodies
narrow heads
pointed snouts
relatively smooth skin
terrestrial

Also available from Stackpole Books and NatureSound Studio:

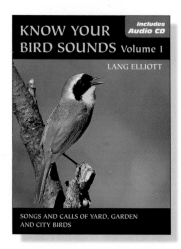

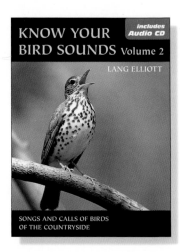

KNOW YOUR BIRD SOUNDS
VOLUMES 1 AND 2
by Lang Elliott

Text and audio guides to the sound repertoires
of common birds of eastern and central North America

- Recordings for a wide variety of songs and calls
- Mnemonics for easy memorization
- Explanations of how each sound is used
- Information on identification and behavior

$19.95, 88 pages, 6 x 8

WWW.STACKPOLEBOOKS.COM
1-800-732-3669